Tobacco Interventions

by
William L. Fibkins

Library of Congress Catalog Card Number 97-69147
ISBN 0-87367-621-1
Copyright © 1997 by the Phi Delta Kappa Educational Foundation
Bloomington, Indiana

Table of Contents

Student Tobacco Abuse

Tobacco use is widespread among teenagers. It is used routinely during the school day by many middle school, junior, and senior high school students on campuses that are labeled "smoke free." Despite all our efforts to provide education and prevention through health classes and information on the dangers of smoking, students continue to smoke. As a result, the use of tobacco among students is a daily concern for many secondary school administrators, teachers, counselors, support staff, parents, and peers of student smokers.

Many students report that they need a cigarette to get temporary relief from the pressures of school and family problems. Many of these teens do have serious personal, family, and school problems; and they are looking for relief in any form in which they can get it. And smoking *does* give them relief. It works! Yet the source of relief — the cigarettes — all too often leads to addiction and more problems. For example, addicted student smokers can not get through the school day without smoking. Some students smoke between each period and go through a pack or more of cigarettes each day.

In *Substance Abuse: The Nation's No. 1 Health Problem* (Horgan 1993), the Robert Wood Johnson Foundation reported that in 1991 almost a third of all Americans aged 12 and older (65 million people) reported smoking. By the time they reach eighth grade, 44% of teens have smoked cigarettes. The study also reported that more than 520,000 deaths each year are linked to the abuse of tobacco and other substances. In addition, a study conducted by the University of Michigan reported that 9% of eighth-graders, 14.6% of tenth-graders, and 19.4% of twelfth-graders smoked cigarettes on a daily basis (*Monitoring the Future Study*, July 1995). Smoking still holds a powerful allure for teenagers.

Student tobacco use is a major discipline and supervision problem for school personnel. The manpower and resources assigned to catching student smokers are costly. Many staff members are entangled in the cycle of catching student smokers, suspending them, readmitting them to school, and then repeating the cycle over and over. Thus tobacco addiction is a huge drain on the increasingly limited resources of the schools.

Tobacco addiction also is very costly to student smokers in terms of risk for school failure and long-term health problems. Tobacco use causes many students to lose valuable class time because of suspensions and absenteeism because of health problems related to smoking. Many student smokers eventually drop out because they are trapped in the addiction cycle and cannot get help to stop or cut back on their smoking.

The report of the Surgeon General of the United States, *Preventing Tobacco Use Among Young People* (1994), reported that teenagers who use tobacco are more likely than those who do not to participate in other significant health-threatening behavior, such as higher-risk sexual intercourse, suicide attempts, and illicit alcohol and drug use. The Centers for Disease Control *Morbidity and Mortality Weekly Report* (November 1996) reported that more than five million Americans now under 18 will die prematurely from smoking.

Clearly, tobacco smoking among teens is a major health issue that needs to be addressed.

In-School Interventions

Tobacco addiction among teenagers can lead to serious illness and an early death. Many of these deaths can be prevented if at-risk teens are involved in smoking cessation programs during the school day.

No other institution in the community is better situated to provide intervention programs to help teenage smokers than is the school. That is where most teen smokers can be found each day, unless they have been suspended, are truant, are ill from heavy tobacco use, or have dropped out because of a continuous cycle of suspensions. Many of the more than five million Americans now under the age of 18 who will die prematurely from smoking are now in our local middle schools, junior high schools, and high schools.

This gives school personnel a unique opportunity to intervene to help these students. Schools also have a great opportunity to help teens with related addictions to alcohol and illicit drugs, as well as with the health, emotional, and academic problems that often accompany their addictions.

Many concerned educators are aware of the alarming tobacco abuse among their students. They observe students at risk of tobacco addiction smoking both on and off school grounds each day. They understand the long-term health consequences to their at-risk students. For concerned educators, student smokers are not statistics that they read about. They know most of the students who use tobacco in their schools.

The obvious student smokers show up to class each day with the smell of smoke on their clothes and a pack of cigarettes sticking out of a coat pocket. Many cough and become increasingly irritable as the class period, in their words, seems to "drag on and never end." Some student smokers do not make it to class because they can not resist the urge to cut class and smoke; their empty classroom chairs mean that the addiction has won out over self-care and learning. There are other student smokers who are less obvious, who do not fit the stereotype of the student rebel who uses tobacco on school grounds to challenge school authorities. These closet smokers do not carry their cigarettes openly for all to see. They often are high-achieving students and athletes — school leaders — who are viewed by peers and faculty as models of health and achievement. But they, too, use cigarettes, and sometimes alcohol and other substances, for relief from pressures. Closet smokers may be less open to intervention because they do not fit the negative stereotype of the student smoker, so they require special intervention to bring them into cessation programs.

For student smokers, the battle rages on each day. Many try to stop smoking on their own. Some succeed, but many more fail. They consider themselves failures who are doomed to a life of addiction.

Yet each day in our schools, there is hope for a change, a new beginning, for student smokers. Remember, the large majority of student smokers want to stop or cut back on their smoking. They acknowledge that it is a deadly habit that may cost them their lives or cause a serious illness. They are looking for a way out. These students need the self-care and self-monitoring skills that can be learned in cessation programs.

Many educators are tired of using outmoded and ineffective intervention practices to help student smokers. They are frustrated with the current practice of suspending smokers, which does little to address the tobacco problem but, instead, disrupts the education process for many students who already are at risk of school failure. They know that many student smokers are beyond the reach of health educators. Educators also know that there are closet smokers among the students who are less obvious but who also need intervention.

Contrary to public opinion that nothing works with addicted students except getting them off the campus, we do know how to help student smokers. We do not have to wait for further research to protect student smokers from an early death or crippling by a smoking-related illness. Forty-four million Americans have quit smoking. Death and illness from tobacco abuse is preventable.

Here is what we know:

1. We know who the majority of student smokers are. They are in our schools on most days.

2. We have four to six hours each school day to intervene to help these student smokers stop or cut back on their smoking.
3. Many of these student smokers are beyond the reach of health classes. They need cessation programs.
4. School-day cessation programs create the conditions for more student smokers, such as closet smokers, to become involved in stopping or cutting back on their habits.
5. School-day cessation programs enable schools to address the student smoking problem as an addiction issue, rather than as a discipline issue.
6. Intervening to help students to resolve nonacademic problems, such as smoking during the school day, is a legitimate role for the schools. It can save lives.

How do educators proceed? Our task as educators is to develop school-day cessation programs that accomplish six important goals:

1. Encourage student smokers to want to change their habit.
2. Provide easily accessible, voluntary cessation programs during the school day for student smokers.
3. Redeploy existing staff members — such as counselors, school nurses, and teachers — to teach cessation classes and to create conditions in the school that can motivate student smokers to seek intervention.
4. Define the cessation program as a normal part of schooling and the education process. It is not an

add-on or a frill, but an essential part of schooling for students. Use a straightforward approach and describe the smoking cessation intervention as a class that student smokers take voluntarily during the school day for a certain number of weeks in order to address their habit, to develop self-care skills, and maybe even to save their lives.

5. Provide ongoing support for recovering student smokers.
6. Use recovering student smokers as peer leaders in cessation programs.

The School-Day Cessation Program

The school-day cessation model is built on the notion that the schools — as overwhelmed as they are — are the natural centers to help at-risk students with tobacco and related addictions. Because at-risk teenagers are in school for much of their daily lives, it follows that the main thrust of prevention and intervention should take place there. No other community institution offers such great access and opportunity for intervention to large numbers of at-risk teens on a regular basis.

Schools not only are encouraged to redeploy existing staff members to plan and deliver intervention services, they also should use such support staff as school monitors and students to serve as sources of information and referral for students addicted to smoking and other substances. Everyone in the school must get on board to help. Each person should be viewed as a source of information and support. In that way, the school becomes a community of responsible and responsive caregivers who are ready and prepared to offer intervention.

There are five understandings that educators should have before establishing school-day cessation programs and creating schools that are truly smoke-free.

1: Understand the six realities of the teenage mind set.

Educators and community leaders need to understand that teenagers view the world differently than do most adults. Getting involved in such risky behavior as tobacco abuse does not seem so risky to most teens. Here is the way they view their world:

- Teens tend to grow up quickly in our culture. As they grow up, they mimic negative adult behaviors, such as smoking. These behaviors often have serious long-term negative health consequences, but the warnings of future ill health seem far-fetched.
- Teens feel invulnerable. They do not believe illness related to their tobacco use will happen to them.
- Teens make decisions based on what is happening to them today. They have a poor sense of long-term consequences. Lecturing to them that tobacco can cause problems later in life does not work.
- Intervention efforts by educators must be rooted in the present and based on real teen experience and behavior.
- In getting help with such problems as smoking, teens depend on support from nonfamily members, such as teachers, support staff, and peers whom they trust and in whom they can confide.
- Teens do not usually seek help with tobacco abuse until they are in a crisis.

2: Understand that schools are the best-positioned institutions to help student smokers stop or cut back on smoking.

Schools are the natural centers for nonacademic intervention for students at risk of tobacco and related addictions. That is where the smokers can be found on most days, in the bathrooms or on the curb across from the school. Because student smokers are in school for most of their day — until the addiction becomes worse and they enter the revolving door of suspensions — it follows that the main thrust of the intervention programs should take place there. This fastback argues that the schools have a mission and legitimate stake in helping students resolve health problems that can kill them.

3: Understand that schools should not consider their education efforts as failures when students continue to smoke tobacco.

Schools are concerned about student tobacco use. They want to help students stop or reduce their smoking. But the approach to the tobacco problem in most schools has been limited to tobacco education in health classes. Some students are difficult to reach; they need cessation programs in addition to education. That is not the fault of the health teachers. Schools should not look at these student smokers as examples of a failed system, but as an opportunity to look for new approaches. When students fail in their academic work, concerned educators look for creative ways to help the students get back on track. We should take the same approach with student smokers and their nonacademic problems.

4: Understand that many student smokers need to learn self-care and the life skills necessary to lead a healthy lifestyle.

Many student smokers do not know how to take care of themselves. They are not skilled at handling stress; they need practice in self-control, making decisions, and solving problems. In addition, many of their adult role models abuse tobacco and other drugs. Students need to learn new ways of self-care and how to become substance free.

5: Understand that concerned teachers, counselors, and school nurses who are respected and trusted by student smokers need to be involved in developing and promoting cessation programs.

Many student smokers resist intervention and the help of outside agencies. They do not feel safe or comfortable attending a cessation program at a local hospital or at the school in the evening with their parents. Seeking help with an addiction is difficult enough. Having to get that help from strangers is not something most teens are willing to undertake. But they are open to the idea of recovery when it comes from people they know and respect. Put simply, they have to be approached by people in whom they can confide, people who will maintain their trust and privacy and who will help them to get involved in a cessation program. Many schools have skilled teachers, counselors, school nurses, support staff, and student peer helpers who are natural-born caregivers. They do know how to get involved and to help at-risk students get the help they need.

With these understandings, educators are ready to establish a rationale, plan, and implement the school-day tobacco cessation program.

Implementing the Program

The first step in implementing a school-day tobacco cessation program is to establish a rationale. Federal law currently prohibits tobacco smoking in all school buildings, and that law does help keep some students from starting the habit. However, the law creates a dilemma for addicted smokers, particularly because many schools do not allow students to leave the building, even for lunch. For example, the smoke-free policies clearly create a dilemma for students who smoke 10 or 11 cigarettes each day, as they probably cannot get through a school day without smoking.

Banning tobacco forces addicted students to break the ban by smoking in the building or by going off campus. Thus the smoke-free policy creates more problems for the schools by increasingly isolating smokers without giving them help. Both the smokers and educators are trapped in a cops-and-robbers game of catching and suspending.

Thus a primary rationale for school-day cessation programs is that they give both student smokers and educators an alternative to suspension that offers intervention and support. The program creates the conditions to help student smokers quit or cut back, instead of creating a dilemma for the addicted student and the school.

There are four steps that educators must consider when planning and implementing the school-day cessation program. Those steps are: 1) defining the program, 2) staffing, 3) recruiting students for the program, and 4) preparing the curriculum.

Defining the Voluntary Cessation Program

Support for the program needs to be generated among faculty, support staff, students, parents, and community members. When the program is announced to the community, care should be taken to define it in a way that encourages such support. Here is an example of such a definition:

> The school is starting a school-day cessation program to teach student smokers how to stop or reduce their smoking. Many students want to quit or cut back on their smoking. We want to help these student smokers by giving them a way out of their deadly habit.
>
> This program also will help reduce the number of students who are suspended for smoking. Student smokers can enroll in the program in lieu of suspension for smoking, or they can volunteer on their own. Students who graduate from the cessation program will have the opportunity to be trained as peer leaders to help in the cessation classes and to recruit other smokers for the program. Our intent is to send a message to student smokers that smoking is a

serious health problem and that the school wants to help them solve this problem.

Although the goal is to enroll every student smoker in the cessation program, we do understand that not all student smokers will avail themselves of this opportunity. We also understand that not every volunteer will complete the program. Some students are severely addicted; for even the most highly motivated of these addicts, stopping or cutting back is going to be a very difficult task.

This program is not a panacea. Some students will continue to smoke in spite of our efforts. With this in mind, the voluntary cessation program must be clearly separated from the disciplinary responses to policy infractions. Student smokers who voluntarily enter the cessation program in lieu of suspension are still subject to discipline if they are caught smoking while in the program, as are all students in the school.

Staffing the Program

The school-day cessation program does not require hiring new staff or using outside consultants. Instead, schools should use the skilled staff they already have. For example, a two-person team consisting of the school nurse and a teacher or counselor can serve as the program's facilitators. These staff members continue in their regular school duties but are given released time to plan and implement the program.

Of course, team members should be educators who have a close working relationship with student smokers and who will be seen by students as people who can help with problems. In addition, administrators should provide opportunities for professional and career development for staff members.

Identifying Students for the Program

The team members will know many of the students who smoke. In addition, they should check the school records for suspensions and visits to the health office to make sure that no student smoker is overlooked. The team members also should ask other teachers, support staff, students, and parents to identify student smokers who may be less obvious. In this way, the team members can develop a list of potential students for the program.

With the list of student smokers, the team is ready to go and "sell" the program. They do this in the way all sales people mount a sales campaign — they talk to student smokers and encourage them to become involved. The team goes where the student smokers are — in the bathrooms and on the curbs across the street from the school — and they tell the student smokers that they want them to volunteer for the program. The team members should expect resistance from the students. But like all good sales people, they should persist.

The team members should give student smokers specific information on how to sign up for the program, when and where it will be held, and the number of sessions that will be involved. They also should explain what will happen in the sessions and what will be expected of students in terms of showing up on time and trying to avoid smoking while in the program. In addition, the educators should assure the students that their privacy will be protected. Students who do volunteer should be encouraged to involve other smokers in the program.

The Cessation Curriculum

When preparing the cessation curriculum, team members must keep their intervention efforts rooted in the present and based on real teen experiences and behavior. Thus the cessation curriculum must not be abstract. That is, it must not consist of lectures about the dangers of smoking or videos of smokers who suffered terrible illness or died. Nor should it include talks from reformed smokers who kicked their habits. Horror stories and tales of failed efforts that led to an early death should be considered taboo.

Instead, the educators should encourage the students to become the lecturers. The students should explain how they began smoking, what smoking does for them, the relationship of their smoking to other substance abuse, and the role of family and friends in their addiction. Students also should describe how they view their future in terms of longevity, health, relationships, and having children. By describing how they began smoking, the student smokers will become more aware of the evolution of their habit.

Team members also should take care to adapt the cessation curriculum to the realities of school life. Schools are busy places with many groups vying for the students' time. Cessation programs need to fit into that busy school schedule without causing conflicts for the students or their teachers. Several points should be kept in mind when designing the curriculum:

1. Be realistic about the number of sessions. Eight to 10 sessions are usually enough to get the curriculum across.

2. Offer one session per week, and vary the time of the sessions. One session per week allows students to try out new behaviors and to complete homework assignments, such as a smoking diary. Varying the time of the meetings helps ensure that students are not being excused from the same class each week.
3. Treat the cessation session as a class, not as a "bull session" with no rules or expectations. It is important for team members to have expectations and a curriculum plan for each session.

Students should be expected to show up on time, to act politely, and to clean up the room after the session. Students need to know that this is a pilot project and has its detractors. Some staff members will be judging the students' behavior and expecting the worst from them. Acting out and causing problems can jeopardize the program and cut off help for smokers in the future. Thus students should be reminded that they have a responsibility and a part to play in making the program work.

Sample Lessons

The curriculum for the tobacco cessation program is not a series of lectures or other teacher-directed activities. The educators in the program are there to encourage the student smokers to discover their own way to break their addiction. However, the classes should have a firm structure to keep them from degenerating into aimless discussion.

Following are eight sample lessons for a cessation program. Each session focuses on a different topic, thus helping the students to examine the various aspects of their tobacco addiction.

Session 1: Welcoming Students

In the first session, the educators first should express their appreciation to the students for volunteering for the program. The educators should emphasize that the work of the group is serious business; the health of many of the members is at risk from smoking. And they should explain that each member of the group can be a major support to helping others to stop smoking. Next they should explain the rules for each session. Following is a sample list of rules:

1. Show up for the group on time.
2. Respect each other. Students may not "put down" others for what they say or do in the session.
3. Keep private what is said in the group. All members' personal stories and lives need to be respected and protected.
4. Each student must sign a contract to stop or reduce smoking.
5. Everyone contributes to bringing snacks and making coffee. We may get pretty anxious in the sessions as we talk about our addictions; munching will help!
6. Each member must keep a smoker's diary. The students must record the number of cigarettes smoked each day, the times they are smoked, and the activity and feelings the student was experiencing when he or she smoked the cigarette. (A sample smoker's diary is included on the following page.)

Session 2: Taking Ownership of Your Smoking

In the second session, the program facilitators should lead the students to talk about how they arrived at the decision to smoke and how they evaluate this decision based on their current information and their personal situations (that is, poor health, coughing, suspensions, and school failure related to frequent suspensions). The facilitators then should provide examples of some steps that students can take to change their habit. A possible

Smoker's Diary

Date: ______________

Time	Feeling/Activity	# of Cigarettes
6:00 - 7:00 a.m.		
7:00 - 8:00		
8:12 - 8:17		
Period 1, 8:21 - 9:05		
Period 2, 9:09 - 9:53		
Period 3, 9:57 - 10:40		
Period 4, 10:44 - 11:27		
Period 5, 11:31 - 12:14		
Period 6, 12:18 - 1:01		
Period 7, 1:05 - 1:49		
Period 8, 1:53 - 2:37		
2:40 - 3:15		
3:15 - 6:00		
6:00 - 8:00		
8:00 - 10:00		
10:00 - 12:00		
12:00 - 2:00		
	Total:	

homework assignment is to have the students observe
how others influence their decision to smoke.

Here are some sample questions that can be used to
facilitate the discussion:

1. Why, where, and when did you start smoking?
2. What do you get out of smoking?
3. Take a look at your smoking diary for the last week.
   What does it tell you about your smoking? Describe your decision-making process when you de-
   cide to light up. What goes on?
4. What role do friends play in your smoking?
5. What role do you play in your friends' smoking?
6. What things in school make you want to smoke?
   A class? A teacher?
7. What things at home make you want to smoke?
8. What happens in your relationships that makes
   you want to smoke?
9. What happens when you try to stop or cut back?
   Within yourself? With your friends? With your
   family?

Session 3: The Relationship Between Self-Image and Smoking

In this session the team helps the students become
aware of the relationship between smoking and their
self-image. The team gets the students to discuss why
they need tobacco, what tobacco does for them, how tobacco is harmful to them, what their self-image would

be like if they did not smoke, and the kind of self-image they want to have. The homework assignment is to write a short description of how others — such as friends, fellow students, teachers, and family — perceive them.

Here are some sample questions that can be used to facilitate the discussion:

1. Talk about your self-image when you first began smoking. For example, did you consider yourself a successful student, good at sports, liked by your peers? Or was your story different?
2. How about the peers you started smoking with? What were they like?
3. How did the teachers and students in the school view you when you first started smoking? Were you "in" or "out"?
4. How about your family? What was your family life like when you first lit up? What did your parents think about you? What was the image your family had in the neighborhood and school? Were they the PTA type?
5. How about now? Has your self-image changed? Has your family's image changed?
6. What does smoking have to do with all of this? Is your image tied to the cigarette? Are you the guy with the smoke in his hand? And sometimes the guy with the smoke and a drink in his hand?
7. Let's talk about your diary for the past few weeks. Take a look at each day. Is your image that of "the smoker"? Is that the way you want it to be?

8. What would you like your image to be? What are your dreams and hopes?

Session 4: The Relationship Between Stress and Smoking

Here the team gets students to identify the stresses in life that contribute to their smoking. Students are reminded that sometimes this discussion brings out very personal data related to family (for example, ongoing family discord) and peer relationships (for example, conflict with a boyfriend). They are asked to maintain the privacy of participants by not speaking about the discussion outside of class.

During this session the students also are given specific techniques on how to relax without a cigarette when these stresses emerge. Their homework is to practice one step to avoid or better handle a stressful situation.

Here are some sample questions that can be used to facilitate the discussion:

1. School can be a stressful place. What in particular do you find stressful in your school day?
2. When you experience stress in school, what happens within you? For example:
   - Does your heart beat faster?
   - Do you find it difficult to concentrate?
   - Do you feel jittery and want to leave the room and the school?
   - Do you get other physical symptoms, for example, diarrhea or stomach pains?
   - Do you perspire?

- Do other students and teachers notice?
- Do you become frightened and want some relief?
- Do you avoid coming to school because it is stressful?
- Do you cut classes to avoid stress?

3. How about home? What kinds of stress occur there and how do you react?
4. How about with friends?
5. How is smoking involved in relieving your stress?
6. Let's talk alternatives to smoking to relieve stress:
   - Deep breathing
   - Meditation
   - Exercise
   - Diet and nutrition
7. How would you like to behave in stressful situations?

Session 5: Learning How to Break the Power of Addiction

In this session, students are asked to suggest concrete methods to help them break the addiction cycle. For example, how can they proceed to make small changes in their daily routine that can help them to be substance free? Their homework is to observe how changing habits is a slow process with many failures, but well worth the effort.

Here are examples of helpful hints that can be used to facilitate discussion:

1. Where in the school can you leave your cigarettes so you cannot get to them so easily? You can get

them at the end of the school day. For example, could you leave them with your homeroom teacher or school counselor?

2. Bring only two cigarettes to school and make a promise not to borrow more from friends.
3. On your free period, do not go to places where you can smoke! Instead, go to a place where you cannot smoke, such as the library or health office, or go to a friend who will encourage you not to smoke.
4. When things get stressful — and they always do — take a deep breath, close your eyes, and visualize a sunset or a peaceful scene. Breathe slowly and repeat five times.
5. On your free period, walk the track or exercise instead of smoking. Find new, healthy locations and activities and get there!
6. Keep putting off having "your" cigarette, one hour at a time, until it becomes a challenge to go longer.
7. Find new ways to occupy your mind and hands: read, do crossword puzzles, meditate, even try homework.
8. Tell your friends about your goal to stop smoking.

At this time, students are also asked to identify their "hot spots." Hot spots are the triggers that set off the need to use the substance. Some examples of student hot spots are: report card time, exam time, school or personal failure, conflict with peers or teachers, conflict with family members, and family or school crisis.

The facilitators also should help the students plan a daily and weekly schedule that will help them to stop or reduce the substance use. Here are some of the elements in this schedule:

- Avoid hot spots in school and at home.
- Avoid peer relationships that encourage substance use.
- Avoid family relationships that encourage substance use.
- Seek peer relationships that do not focus on substance use.
- Seek positive school experiences.
- Set specific targets (for example, "I will smoke only one cigarette per day in the coming week").

Here is an example of one day's schedule:

- Before school: I will not have a cigarette before homeroom.
- Period 1, English: I will not cut English to have a cigarette with Maureen.
- Period 4, social studies: I will not go to the boy's bathroom between periods to smoke with Todd.
- Period 5, free period: I will go to the nurse's office to attend the 5-Hour-a-Day Program to help students stop or reduce smoking during the school day. The nurse has gum and snacks to keep me busy.
- Period 6, lunch: I will not go off campus to eat at the deli with Frank and Jenny. I will eat in the cafeteria so I won't smoke.
- After school: I will join the soccer team to keep busy.
- Evening: I will study at the community library so I avoid being around my parents' smoking and

drinking. I will call my 5-Hour Support Group if I need to talk about my problems or feel the need to have a cigarette. I am available to offer help and support to my peers in the 5-Hour Program.
- Weekends: I will not attend parties where my peers drink and smoke. I will get involved in activities with my 5-Hour peers.

Session 6: Learning New Ways to Reward Yourself

In the sixth session, the team helps students to focus on ways to reward themselves other than by smoking. Students are asked to identify activities other than smoking that they enjoy and find meaningful. The homework assignment is for students to write a one-page essay on how they can spend more of their time pursuing these life-giving activities.

Here are examples of questions that can be used to facilitate discussion:

1. Tell us about your hopes and dreams.
2. Do you feel they are going to come true, that you will live that dream?
3. How have your failures put a damper on your dreams? Have you, like so many others, settled for less?
4. What people — parents, teachers, friends — have put down your dreams? What were the words they used? Were they hurtful? What do you do when you are hurt?

5. Have you turned to tobacco and other substances when you felt your dreams slipping away? Did that relief help, or was it temporary and sometimes a problem itself?
6. Do you believe in the notion that we can begin again and can make small gains, small steps, toward our dreams?
7. Let's begin now. What small steps can you take toward having that dream?
8. What rewards can you give yourself for trying anew? Instead of a pack of cigarettes or a six-pack, how about a ticket to the ballet, a walk on the beach, a new sweater or CD?
9. How about getting involved with an adult who can help you reach your goal, someone who can value your dream and help open doors? Do you have someone in mind?

Session 7: Assessing Your New Learning

As they approach the ending of the cessation program, the team gets students to assess what they have learned. Have they been able to stop or cut back on their smoking? Do they have fewer class cuts? Have they become more aware of how to avoid or better handle the stresses in their lives that have led to smoking? Has the cessation program prompted them to seek out new relationships with non-smokers? Have they become more aware of those activities that can give them a feeling of purpose in life? Do they have new sources of support from fellow students in the program and the team facilitators? Are they informed about resources in the community that can offer them support for related health, family, and personal problems, such as alcohol and drug addiction, sexual concerns, eating disorders?

Here are some sample questions that can be used to facilitate discussion:

1. Have you assumed responsibility for your smoking and other abusive behaviors?
2. Have you been able to stop or cut back on your smoking?
3. What new learning and behaviors helped you?
4. Do you have fewer detentions and suspensions?
5. Do you have a better awareness of the stresses that trigger your smoking and how you can better handle those stresses without lighting up?
6. Do you have better insight into your own self-image, and have you learned new ways to improve your image?
7. Have you refocused your hopes and dreams and set up a system of self-rewards for small gains you make toward your dreams?
8. Have you learned that changing an addiction is difficult, that you may have relapses? Do you have a support group available to help you in the future?

Session 8: Setting Goals

In this final session, students are asked to set specific goals for stopping or reducing their smoking. They also are invited to sign up for a training program to become peer leaders for student smokers who have volunteered for the next cessation class. The task of a peer leader is to be available for support and information during and after school for small groups of cessation class members.

Conclusion

School-day cessation programs are not a panacea. Students addicted to tobacco are difficult to reach, and many approaches and resources are needed to get the job done. However, these programs can be an important tool as schools implement the federal ban on smoking tobacco in schools. An effective school-based cessation program can provide a positive alternative to which student smokers can turn to for help. Cessation programs also serve as an important support for education and prevention efforts offered by health classes at the middle school, junior high, and high school levels.

Schools do not have to make major changes in their daily schedules and the schedules of students in order to put a school-day cessation program in place. Nor are such programs expensive. The resources needed for the program are, in fact, very modest. Generally, such programs need only: release time for staff, a comfortable room, minimal release time for students, and a small budget for snacks.

The leadership role of the school nurse, counselors, and teachers is important. It is these educators who will encourage students to volunteer for the cessation program. Many schools already have such skilled staff in place. In addition, the leadership and support of school administrators is vital for the school-day cessation program to succeed.

However, schools by themselves cannot succeed in the effort to help student smokers. They need the aid and support of others in the community. Health care professionals, businesses, and religious and civic organizations in the community must play a part in education and prevention. For example, health and law enforcement agencies can work to monitor the sale of tobacco to teenagers. Community health agencies can provide cessation classes, counseling, and access to evening rehabilitation programs for related addictions. Schools can provide the necessary bridge to community resources for student smokers who are difficult to reach by clearly identifying sources of help and ways of reaching them.

The schools offer the best opportunity for helping student smokers, because that is where they can be found. Many student smokers want to quit smoking, but first they need to learn better ways to handle the stresses and problems in their lives. Helping these students to address their smoking and to develop healthy habits is an important and legitimate role for the schools. Cessation programs can save lives.

Resources

Readers who are interested in developing a school-day cessation program will need additional information in order to develop the program that best fits the needs of their individual school. While this fastback can serve as a starting point for busy educators, it is not intended to answer every question about school-day cessation programs. Following is a list of additional resources, including books and organizations, as well as the addresses of schools that have implemented such programs.

Publications

Dryfoos, Joy G. *Full-Service Schools: A Revolution in Health and Social Services for Children, Youth and Families.* San Francisco: Jossey-Bass, 1994.

This book makes the case for school-based intervention programs to address the non-academic needs of students.

Fibkins, William L. *The Empowering School: Getting Everyone on Board to Help Teenagers.* San Jose, Calif.: Resource Publications, 1995.

Explains how to introduce school-based tobacco, alcohol, and drug intervention programs and how to train professional facilitators.

Fibkins, William L. *The Teacher-as-Helper Training Manual*. San Jose, Calif.: Resource Publications, 1997.

Intended for secondary school administrators and teacher leaders, this book explains how to train teachers to intervene to help at-risk students in such areas as tobacco, alcohol and drug abuse.

Horgan, Constance. *Substance Abuse: The Nation's No. 1 Health Problem*. Princeton, N.J.: Robert Wood Johnson Foundation, 1993.

Office on Smoking and Health, National Center for Chronic Disease Prevention and Health Promotion. *Morbidity and Mortality Weekly Report*. Atlanta, Ga.: Centers for Disease Control.

Preventing Tobacco Use Among Young People: A Report of the Surgeon General of the United States. Atlanta, Ga.: U.S. Department of Health, Public Health Service, Centers for Disease Control and Prevention, National Center for Chronic Disease Prevention and Health Promotion, Office on Smoking and Health, 1994.

University of Michigan Institute for Social Research and National Institute on Drug Abuse. *Monitoring the Future Study*. Rockville, Md.: U.S. Department of Human Services, Public Health Service, National Institute of Health, National Institute on Drug Abuse.

This is an annual publication.

Organizations

American Association of School Administrators
1801 North Moore Street
Arlington, VA 22209
(703) 528-0700
Provides information on effective school health programs.

American Lung Association of Minnesota
490 Concordia Avenue
St. Paul, MN 55102-2441
1-800-642-LUNG
Resource center for Tobacco-Free Teens Project. Contact Allen Terwedo.

American Medical Association, Smokeless States Program
Department of Preventive Medicine and Public Health
515 North State Street
Chicago, IL 60610
(312) 464-5957
The goal of the program is to reduce tobacco use among Americans, particularly children and youth. Contact Thomas P. Houston, M.D.

Boulder County Department of Health
3450 Broadway
Boulder, CO 80304
(303) 441-1284
The department is involved in establishing school-based tobacco intervention programs and teacher training. Contact Cheryl Christensen.

Carnegie Corporation of New York
437 Madison Avenue
New York, NY 10022
(212) 371-3200
Publishes the *Carnegie Quarterly*, which addresses recent research and program development in adolescent health issues.

The Center for Empowerment
22 South Gillette Avenue
Bayport, NY 11705
(516) 472-1207
The center offers training for educators and student leaders on developing school-based intervention programs.
Contact William L. Fibkins.

Center for Substance Abuse Prevention,
    Teen Smoking Project
821 First Street, NE, Suite 510
Washington, DC 20002
1-800-937-6727.

Davis County Tobacco Intervention Program
Davis County Courthouse Annex, Box 618
Farmington, UT 84025
(801) 451-3322
Contact Kevin Condra.

Division of Adolescent and School Health Promotion
U.S. Department of Health and Human Services,
    Centers for Disease Control
4770 Buford Highway, NE, Mailstop K-33
Atlanta, GA 30341-3724
(770) 488-5345
Resource center for information on at-risk youth and tobacco intervention programs. Contact Linda Crossett.

Health Science Center, Office of School Health
University of Colorado
4200 East 9th Avenue, C-287
Denver, CO 80262
(303) 270-7437
Resource and training center for school-based tobacco intervention projects. Contact Marily Harmacek.

Join Together
441 Stuart Street
Boston, MA 02116
(617) 437-1500
A resource center sponsored by the Robert Wood Johnson Foundation to address substance abuse among young people.

National Clearinghouse for Alcohol and Drug
  Information
P.O. Box 2345
Rockville, MD 20847-2345
1-800-729-6686
NCADI is the information service for the Center for Substance Abuse Prevention.

National School Boards Association
1680 Duke Street
Alexandria, VA 22314
(703) 838-6722
Resource center for school health programs. Contact Betty Poehlmann.

Project ASSIST, Community Health Cooperative
P.O. Box 11834
Charlotte, NC 28220
(704) 442-9629
Project ASSIST works with schools to address teen to-
bacco issues. Contact Glenna Davenport-Cook.

State of Maine Project ASSIST
151 Capitol Street, State House Station 11
Augusta, ME 04333
(207) 287-5180
Contact Chris Stark.

State of North Carolina Project ASSIST
153 East Lindsay Street
Greensboro, NC 27401.

Utah Department of Health
288 North 1460 West, Box 14872
Salt Lake City, UT 84114-2872
(801) 538-6101
Resource and training center for school-based tobacco
intervention projects. Contact Kristine Foulke.

School-Based Tobacco Intervention Programs

Fryeburg Academy
152 Main Street
Fryeburg, ME 04037
(207) 935-2318
Contact Ellen Raynsford.

Shoreham-Wading River High School
Route 25A
Shoreham, NY 11788
(516) 821-8140
Contact Principal Joseph Haywood and School Nurse
Lorrain Esper.

State College Area High School
653 Westerly Parkway
State College, PA 16803
(717) 231-1157
Contact Principal Ron Pifer and School Nurse Nikki
Silvis.

Westhampton Beach High School
Lilac Road
Westhampton Beach, NY 11979
(516) 288-3800
Contact Guidance Counselor Vivian Hudson and School
Nurse Pam Abbatiello.